Smithsonian

LITTLE EXPLORER

A 4D BOOK

DASHING DRAGONFLIES

by Megan Cooley Peterson

PEBBLE

a capstone imprint

① Ask an adult to download the app.

 Capstone 4D
Education

② Scan any page with the star.

③ Enjoy your cool stuff!

— OR —

Use this password at capstone4D.com

dragonflies.03444

Little Explorer is published by Pebble,
1710 Roe Crest Drive, North Mankato, Minnesota 56003
www.mycapstone.com

The name of the Smithsonian Institution and the sunburst
logo are registered trademarks of the Smithsonian Institution.
For more information, please visit www.si.edu.

Library of Congress Cataloging-in-Publication Data
Names: Peterson, Megan Cooley, author.
Title: Dashing dragonflies : a 4D book / by Megan Cooley
   Peterson.
Description: North Mankato, Minnesota : Pebble, [2019] | Series:
   Little entomologist 4D | Audience: Age 4-8. | Audience: K to
   Grade 3. | Includes bibliographical references and index.
Identifiers: LCCN 2018041895 | ISBN 9781977103444 (library
   binding) | ISBN 9781977105714 (paperback) | ISBN
   9781977103505 (ebook pdf)
Subjects: LCSH: Dragonflies—Juvenile literature.
Classification: LCC QL520 .P494 2019 | DDC 595.7/33—dc23
LC record available at https://lccn.loc.gov/2018041895

Editorial Credits
Abby Colich, editor; Kyle Grenz, designer; Kelly Garvin,
media researcher; Tori Abraham, production specialist

Our very special thanks to Gary Hevel, Public Information
Officer (Emeritus), Entomology Department, at the Smithsonian
National Museum of Natural History. Capstone would also like
to thank Kealy Gordon, Product Development Manager, and the
following at Smithsonian Enterprises: Ellen Nanney, Licensing
Manager; Brigid Ferraro, Vice President, Education and Consumer
Products; and Carol LeBlanc, Senior Vice President, Education and
Consumer Products.

Image Credits
Alamy: Andre Seale, 13, blickwinkel, 22; Minden Pictures/Alex
Huizinga, 29; Shutterstock: Abeselom Zerit, 9, alslutsky, 2, 14
(bottom), Arto Hakola, 15, 17, Birds and Dragons, 7, By, 14 (top),
Davidolfi, 23, Deer worawut, 27, Hintau Aliaksei, 5, Kaettisak
pongpat, cover, Kazakova Maryia, 8, Lewis Tse Pui Lung, 19, Nancy
Bauer, 26, Richard A McMillin, 1, Samib123, 25, Simon_g, 21, suradech
sribuanoy, 11

Printed and bound in the United States of America.
062019   002206

Table of Contents

Meet the Dragonflies

Have you ever seen a dragonfly? You were probably near a pond or stream. Dragonflies love water. Females lay their eggs in water. Dragonflies dart and dive through the air as they look for food to eat. Some dragonflies eat hundreds of other bugs every day. They help lower the numbers of mosquitoes, flies, and other pests. Dragonflies are also food for birds, fish, bats, and lizards. More than 3,000 species of dragonflies live around the world.

DID YOU KNOW?

Don't let the name fool you! Dragonflies are not flies.

A Dragonfly's Body

Dragonflies are insects. They have two pairs of wings. They have six legs. Their antennae are tiny. Dragonflies see with big eyes. They use their sight to find and catch food. They can see in almost every direction. They also see in color.

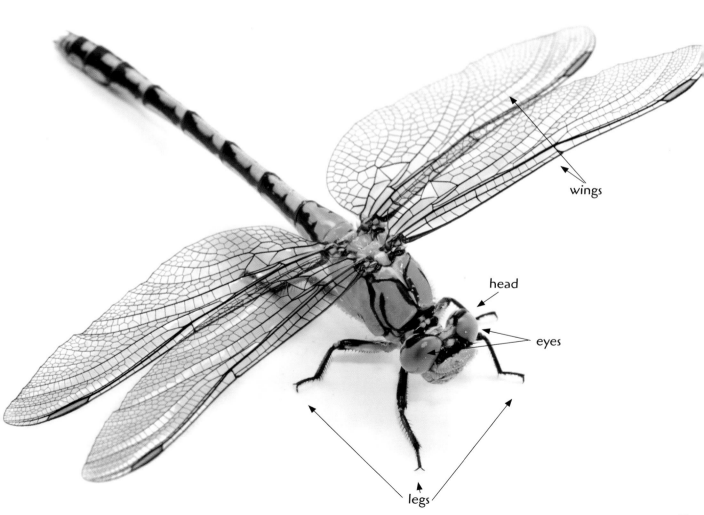

wings

head

eyes

legs

5

King Skimmers

Number of species: 56
Found: Worldwide except Antarctica
Length: 1.8 to 2.2 inches (4.6 to 5.6 centimeters)

King skimmers skim the tops of ponds, lakes, and marshes. Females drag their bodies through the water to lay eggs. Skimmers perch on plants. They soak up warmth from the sun. They also wait for a bug to fly by. Then they shoot into the air to grab the prey.

DID YOU KNOW?

Roseate skimmers stand out in a crowd! Males have purple and pink bodies. Females and young roseates are brown.

7

Whitetails

Number of species: 2
Found: North and Central America
Length: 1.8 to 2.8 inches (4.6 to 7.1 cm)

It's easy to spot a whitetail dragonfly. Male common whitetails have a chalky white body. They wave it in the air to chase off other males.

A female lays eggs quickly. One female can lay 2,000 eggs a minute. Her body can store a lot of eggs.

Life of a Dragonfly

Dragonflies start life as eggs. Eggs hatch into nymphs. Nymphs live in water. They look like adults without wings. Nymphs molt many times before they become adults.

adult

molting

eggs

nymph

Rainpool Gliders

Number of species: 2
Found: Worldwide except Antarctica
Length: 1.7 to 2 inches (4.3 to 5.1 cm)

The rain has just stopped. Rainpool gliders get to work. They lay eggs in ponds and puddles after it rains. The nymphs grow quickly, before the water dries up.

Frequent Fliers

The wandering glider is also called the globe skimmer. It migrates the longest of any insect. Each year, wandering gliders in India fly across the Indian Ocean. They follow the rain all the way to east Africa. Then they go back home. The trip is thousands of miles long.

wandering glider

Wandering gliders and spot-winged gliders look alike. Spot-winged gliders have spots at the base of their hind wings. Wandering gliders have clear wings. Both of these dragonflies are great gliders.

Pondhawks

Number of species: 10
Found: North, Central, and South America
Length: 1.5 to 1.9 inches (3.8 to 4.8 cm)

Watch out for hungry pondhawks! These dragonflies attack any insect they can find. They even eat larger dragonflies.

Flame-tailed pondhawks are hard to miss. Males have dark blue and purple faces. Their bodies are bright red. Females are gold or brown. They have a yellow stripe between their wings.

DID YOU KNOW?

Dragonflies have sharp mandibles. They work like teeth. The mandibles have jagged edges like a knife.

How Dragonflies Hunt

Dragonflies catch up to 95 percent of the prey they go after. That's more than sharks or lions. Dragonflies hunt by perching or flying. Perchers rest on a plant. They watch for bugs and then take off to catch them. Fliers don't stop to rest. They fly almost nonstop, eating bugs midair.

Saddlebags

Number of species: 21
Found: Worldwide except Antarctica
Length: 2 inches (5.1 cm) or longer

Saddlebags make their own shade. They have round spots on their hind wings. The spots look like saddlebags on a horse. When it's hot, saddlebags perch on a branch. They spread their wings and curl up under the shade of their spots.

Dragonfly or Damselfly?

Dragonflies look a lot like damselflies. You can tell them apart by how they perch. Dragonflies spread their wings when they rest. Damselflies fold their wings. Dragonflies are also larger. Damselflies have thinner bodies.

dragonfly

damselfly

Black saddlebags often look for food in swarms. They even swarm with other dragonflies, such as the common green darner.

Small Pennants

Number of species: 8
Found: North America
Length: 1 to 1.7 inches (2.5 to 4.3 cm)

Small pennants land on the tops of tall plants. They hold their hind wings straight out. They hold their front wings up at an angle. They look like flags, or pennants, as they wave in the breeze.

Boo! The Halloween pennant is black and orange. It flies mostly in the summer months. It flutters like a butterfly.

DID YOU KNOW?

Dragonflies first appeared about 300 million years ago. That's even before the dinosaurs. Early dragonflies had huge wingspans. Some were 2 feet (0.6 meter) wide!

Pygmyflies

Number of species: 6
Found: Asia and Australia
Length: 0.3 to 0.7 inch (0.8 to 1.8 cm)

Don't blink! You might miss the pygmyflies. These dragonflies are some of the smallest in the world. The scarlet dwarf measures just 0.6 inch (1.5 cm) long. Males have a red body and red eyes.

On hot days you might spot a scarlet dwarf doing a handstand! They point their bodies toward the sun. This helps keep some dragonflies from getting too hot.

Freaky Fliers

Dragonflies are some of the best fliers on Earth. They can move each wing on its own. They fly forward, backward, and sideways. They even hover like a helicopter. Dragonflies are also the fastest flying insects. They can fly up to 35 miles (56 km) per hour! That's faster than most dogs can run.

Flutterers

Number of species: 25
Found: Africa, Asia, and Australia
Length: 0.9 to 1.6 inches (2.3 to 4.1 cm)

Flutterers don't soar like other dragonflies. They flutter! The graphic flutterer from Australia looks like a work of art. Spots of dark brown cover bright yellow wings.

The phantom flutterer has a bluish body. Its clear wings have splashes of metallic purple or pink. This dragonfly lives throughout Africa.

Darners

Number of species: 480
Found: Worldwide except Antarctica
Length: 2 to 3 inches (5.1 to 7.6 cm)

Darner dragonflies are named for a kind of sewing needle. Females have points at the ends of their bodies. They use these points to cut through plants to lay eggs. Darners are also called hawkers. Like hawks, they are skilled hunters.

The blue-eyed darner's bright eyes can't be missed. This dragonfly, like other darners, catches bugs midair. Its strong mandibles bite into prey.

DID YOU KNOW?
Some darner nymphs hunt tadpoles.

22

Spiketails

Number of species: 55
Found: Worldwide except Antarctica
Length: 2 to 3.5 inches (5.1 to 8.9 cm)

Spiketails spend most of their time near streams. These dragonflies have dark bodies with yellow marks. They can have blue or green eyes.

Females have a spike on the ends of their bodies. To lay eggs, females find a shallow stream. They stab their spikes into mud. They look like sewing needles as they bob up and down. The mud keeps the eggs safe.

The golden-ringed dragonfly is a member of the spiketail family.

Clubtails

Number of species: 900
Found: Worldwide except Antarctica
Length: 1.5 to 3.5 inches (3.8 to 8.9 cm)

Clubtails are easy to spot. They have large bulges at the ends of their bodies. They also have wide-set eyes.

The dragonhunter isn't afraid to eat dangerous foods. It hunts monarch butterflies. Monarchs eat milkweed. Milkweed is a poisonous plant. This clubtail dragonfly knows which parts of the monarch are safe to eat.

monarch butterfly on milkweed

DID YOU KNOW?

Clubtails live in shaded areas alongside rivers and streams.

Emeralds

Number of species: 165
Found: Worldwide
Length: 1.7 to 2.7 inches (4.3 to 6.9 cm)

Emerald dragonflies have bright green eyes. Some have bright green or bronze bodies. They look like flying pieces of metal! Others are dark and black. An emerald's body can be thinner than other dragonflies. It flies for hours looking for prey. It catches bugs midair and gobbles them up.

Glossary

antenna (an-TE-nuh)—a feeler on an insect's head

gill (GIL)—a body part some insects use to breathe underwater

mandible (MAN-duh-buhl)—strong mouthparts used to chew

migrate (MYE-grate)—to move from one place to another at different times of the year

molt (MOLT)—to shed an outer layer of skin

nymph (NIMF)—a young form of an insect; nymphs change into adults by shedding their skin many times

perch (PURCH)—to stand on the edge of something

prey (PRAY)—an animal hunted by another animal for food

skim (SKIM)—to glide or skip along the surface of the water

species (SPEE-seez)—a group of living things that can reproduce with one another

swarm (SWARM)—to gather or fly close together in a large group

Critical Thinking Questions

1. Dragonflies are some of the deadliest hunters on Earth. How do their body parts help them hunt prey?

2. Could dragonflies survive without water? Explain why or why not.

3. Dragonfly nymphs molt many times before they become adults. Why do some species take longer than others to reach adulthood? How does their habitat affect their growth?

Read More

Black, Nessa. *Dragonflies.* Creepy Crawlies. Mankato, Minn.: Amicus Ink, 2019.

Hansen, Grace. *Becoming a Dragonfly.* Changing Animals. Minneapolis: Abdo Kids, 2017.

Perish, Patrick. *Dragonflies.* Insects up Close. Minneapolis: Bellwether Media, 2018.

Internet Sites

Use FactHound to find Internet sites related to this book.

Visit *www.facthound.com*

Just type in 9781977103444 and go.

Check out projects, games and lots more at
www.capstonekids.com

Index